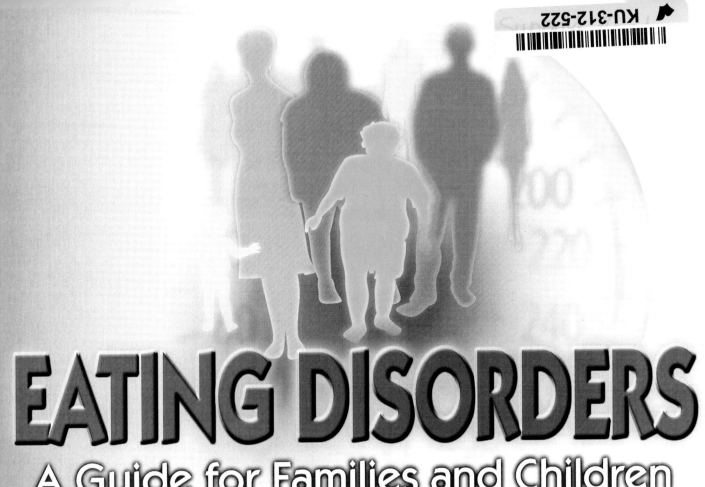

EATING DISORDERS
A Guide for Families and Children

Valerie J. Elsbree

Foreword by
Sarah Ferguson
The Duchess of York

Valerie J. Elsbree

Ms Elsbree, MSW, LCSW, CAP is a licensed psychotherapist with a Master's degree in Social Work, a license in clinical social work and is a Certified Addictions Professional, Certified in Addictions Counseling and Addictions Studies. She received her degrees from Florida International University, The Union Institute of Miami, University of Miami, and The Addictions Institute. Ms. Elsbree is on the Board of Directors for Food Addicts Anonymous

For almost 20 years, Ms. Elsbree has worked with children, adolescents and adults in the Mental Health and Substance Abuse fields. She has worked extensively with individuals addicted to food, alcohol, drugs, gambling, sex and codependency. Ms. Elsbree has worked with and advocated for the homeless population and was Director of a homeless program with over 300 beds. She has authored grants in the US to further the cause of the underserved, including women and their children, to receive shelter, food, therapy, and education, which would enable them to better their lives and to become self-sufficient. A highly respected therapist specializing in addiction, Ms. Elsbree is in private practice in Ft Lauderdale, Florida. She is a freelance writer and has a column in a national magazine for people recovering from addictions where she attempts to dispel rumors and answers questions that have plagued us about addiction.

How to use this book

Read the text and study the illustrations with the child/children. Each illustration reflects the symptoms listed at the top of each page and depicts a typical scenario of family life with an eating disordered individual.

Under the heading, 'Speaking with Your Child', suggestions have been made to encourage open dialogue about the symptoms they are seeing and experiencing with their loved one.

Try to explain more about the disease by using the colorful pictures and Facts included at the bottom of each page. Glossary words are also located at the bottom of each page to help make explanations easier for all readers.

Children want to know and understand why their loved ones behave and react in certain ways. By encouraging open communication between them and your loved one with an eating disorder, you are not only educating them, you are also bringing them closer together. Taking a step further, by talking to a medical or other healthcare professional, the dialogue opens further to greatly improve chances of recovery.

Design and artwork by

SMK Design

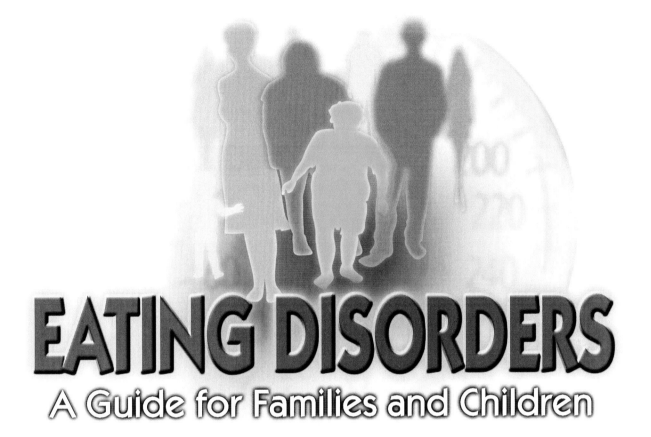

EATING DISORDERS
A Guide for Families and Children

ISBN: 978-1-873413-49-4

North American address:
1095 Jupiter Park Drive
Suite 7
Jupiter, FL 33458
USA

Tel: (561) 697 -1116
Email: meritpi@aol.com

European address:
50 Highpoint
Heath Road, Weybridge
Surrey KT13 8TP
UK

Tel: (44) (0) 1932 844526
Email: merituk@aol.com

Web: www.meritpublishing.com

merit
PUBLISHING
INTERNATIONAL

Contents

Sarah Ferguson, The Duchess of York

Foreword

It may seem ironic that I should be offering advice on weight. After all, I have struggled with my weight for much of my life.

For me, as for many people, being overweight was symptomatic of deeper issues. When I was 12-years-old I began misusing food to cope with sadness following my parent's divorce. In moments of weakness, bingeing enabled me to swallow my emotions, a strategy that seemed to work until my marriage thrust me onto the world stage. The frequency of my bingeing escalated under the pressure of public life and with that my weight ballooned.

I was well into my 30's before I managed to get control. It was with the help of WeightWatchers® that I learned the ins and outs of healthy eating and discovered how to break the emotional eating habits that perpetuated my weight problem.

As you will learn in this book, it is impossible to generalize about the causes and treatments for food addictions. Each individual is unique in both their struggle and the best approach to recovery. Reading these chapters will you give you the facts and insight you need to make informed decisions.

Mine was a long and lonely downward spiral that was fueled by hurt and low esteem. But I am proof that there is hope; provided the right information and compassionate support, in time I was able to overcome my eating problem. In doing so, my health and quality of life improved immeasurably.

You can succeed, too. I urge you to find the courage in your heart to start your journey toward recovery now.

Sarah Ferguson, The Duchess of York

Introduction

You Are Not Alone

Although I am a licensed psychotherapist specializing in eating disorders and addictions, my additional expertise on the subjects truly comes from personal experience as an eating disordered person, and one who has had these genes passed on from my grandparents and parents who suffered from eating disorders.

Eating disorders not only affect the person afflicted with it, but also their spouses, partners, children, family, and friends. This is a progressive disease, which means it gets worse over time without help. Obesity, in particular, is becoming an international plague.

Children should especially be helped to understand why their loved one with an eating disorder is behaving in certain ways. Children are open and vulnerable and benefit from information and knowledge that reassure them and help them feel safe and secure in their understanding of their loved ones' problems. They benefit, as well, from a heightened awareness of the importance of a balanced way of eating and exercising for their own personal choices in these areas.

Many years ago, tipping the scale at just under 300lbs (21.43st or 136.3kl.), there were several things that occurred in my life that, shall we say, helped me "hit bottom" with my addiction to food. The one incident that stands out from the rest is when my first born child began school. It was in 1978 and a very exciting time for our family when Christopher started school. For the first few days, my husband and I walked Christopher to his classroom together and picked him up at the end of the day. By the second week of school, due to work obligations, my husband could no longer join us so I took Christopher each morning by myself and collected him each afternoon. At the beginning of the third week, Christopher tearfully stated, "Mommy, please stay in the car and don't walk me to my classroom anymore." When I asked him why, he stated, "The kids all laugh and make fun of you because you're fat." After dropping him off that day, I drove home sobbing, feeling ashamed and as if my heart had broken.

Some time later, it was our daughter Nicole's turn to begin school. By then, however, I had the drop off and collection from the school rehearsed and it went easily, meaning that although I could be certain she arrived safely at her classroom, I could also ensure that no one would see me. Part of my disease of addiction to food was to arrange or adapt my life, or those of my family members, to not interfere with the way I was eating.

This was the beginning of the end of the constant overeating that was causing me to have physical ailments and other medical problems that threatened my life. It led me to treatment, recovery and a large weight loss that also threatened my life. Following my own recovery, I made a decision to return to college to get the education needed to work in this field and help others with the same problems.

In the United States alone, approximately 66% of people are either overweight or obese. In the UK, the prevalence rates for overweight and obesity are among the highest in Europe and a large percentage of heart attacks in Europe are actually due to abdominal obesity. Obesity and other eating disorders are rising to epidemic proportions along with associated problems such as, heart disease, diabetes, arthritis, and more.

Unless serious and quick actions are taken to reduce obesity, the steady rise in living long lives that we have become used to seeing in the Modern era will soon come to an end[6]. If the negative effect of obesity on life expectancy continues to get worse and today's trends show it will, the progress we've made over many decades of living healthy, long lives will reverse quickly[1].

Shockingly, the current generation is the first generation that may not outlive their parents. If nothing is done, the children of today will continue to be unhealthy and live even shorter lives than their parents.

1. Olshansky, S.J., D. J. Passaro, Hershow, R.C. Layden, J. (2005). A Potential Decline in Life Expectancy in the United States in the 21st Century. New England Journal of Medicine, 352, 1138-1146.

A Message of Hope

The hope for successful recovery from an eating disorder is promising when one chooses to use the help available today, some of which may include a complete medical examination, a nutritionist, counseling or therapy, psychiatric evaluation, and medication management. The levels of care available may include outpatient, day treatment, intensive outpatient, residential (rehab), and extended care/aftercare. The 12-Step recovery programs have proven to be positive support networks for those dealing with an eating disorder.

Eating disorders often come from a combination of psychological, interpersonal and social environments. Feelings of low self-esteem, depression, anxiety, and loneliness, as well as troubled family and personal relationships, may add to the development of an eating disorder. Statistics are very high linking sexual abuse and eating disorders. Internationally, many cultures think thinness and the "perfect body" is the most important goal to have. This way of thinking often plays a part in the beginning of an eating disorder, as no human being can be perfect!

Extreme dieting, bingeing, and purging (making one self-vomit after eating) are ways in which some people deal with painful emotions and feel as if they are in control of their lives. At the same time, these behaviors can weaken physical, mental and emotional health, self-esteem/self-worth, and a feeling of self-control.

It is important to realize that not all under or over weight people have eating disorders. For a health care professional to find out if a person has an eating disorder, the individual needs to have behaviors, thoughts, and feelings that last over a certain period of time, contributing to an unhealthy relationship with food. Research suggests that genetics, environment and behavior are key components that determine the size of a person.

Often, people with eating disorders feel like they are different or their problems are unique and different from others and that no one understands their daily struggles with food. Many times they isolate themselves from others and feel hopeless about their situation, and live with feelings of shame and guilt about their behaviors with food.

Those suffering from an eating disorder need loving, caring and compassionate people around them who show they care and with whom they can openly laugh. The love, acceptance and support of a child can also open our minds and our hearts. This book aims to address the questions of children and families affected by eating disorders and it will help them to become empowered through knowledge and truthful answers.

Reading and identifying with people of all ages and lifestyles and real-life stories in this book are an excellent ways for the eating disordered person and their loved ones to see and relate, perhaps for the first time, their behaviors around food. If you, or a loved one or friend are affected, you will see that you or they are not alone, that individual situations are not hopeless and there is help nearby followed by recovery.

It is my aim to open minds about eating disorders and in turn, create a foundation for dialogue with your loved ones. Very importantly, this book can also be a starting place for dialogue with doctors and other health care professionals to begin the recovery process.

Family members who have been living with fear, worry and feelings of powerlessness about themselves or their loved one suffering with an eating disorder will be relieved that there is help available. In addition to removing the stigma attached to eating disorders, the objective of this book is to provide eating disordered persons, their families, children and friends with the knowledge, strength, and hope needed to bring this secretive disease out of the darkness and into the light, where they will find help for all who have been affected.

Valerie J. Elsbree

Obesity and *Morbid Obesity

My father eats all the time. He eats while he's cooking, then he eats dinner with us. Sometimes, he eats our leftovers.

Speaking with your child

Does it bother you that your dad eats so much? Are you worried about him because he is overweight? How do you feel when he eats your leftovers?

GLOSSARY WORDS:

* **Morbid Obesity** - weighing approximately twice the ideal weight.
* **Guilty** - a feeling or emotion that may occur when having done something wrong.
* **Disgusted** - feeling a strong dislike towards.
* **Self-esteem** - a person's sense of personal worth that comes from his/her inner thoughts and feelings.
* **Obesity** - an accumulation of too much fat in the body.
* **Purge** - make oneself vomit.

FACTS

People with Binge Eating Disorders eat often and until they are uncomfortably or painfully full but do not *purge to rid excess calories. They eat when they are not physically hungry and feel *guilty and *disgusted with themselves after eating. They tend to have difficulty knowing what they are feeling and have low *self-esteem.

Food as an *Addiction

Auntie Li went to get help because she was very heavy. She stayed in a place for many days because she can't stop eating sweets. They taught Auntie how to eat right. Auntie says if she eats even one bite of cake she can't stop eating the whole cake.

Speaking with your child

Do you feel bad that Auntie can't have cake on your birthday?
How can you and I help Auntie to eat the right things when she visits us?
We have to tell Auntie she looks great so she feels good about herself.

GLOSSARY WORDS:

* **Refined carbohydrates** - sugars, flours, starches, like cake, cookies, ice cream, candy.
* **Addiction** - to give oneself up to a strong habit.
* **Irresistible** - so desirable that it is very difficult to resist.

FACTS

Experts in the field of eating disorders agree that when *refined carbohydrates are eaten they can set up an addictive process like the one with the alcoholic, heroin addict, or cocaine addict, Stark (2001)[2]. Once eaten, some describe the cravings as a physical and mental state that is so strong that it is *irresistible; Omitting these refined carbohydrates from one's daily food intake can eliminate these strong cravings and is one part of dealing with food addiction.

2. Lindeman M.; Stark K. (2001) Emotional Eating and Eating Disorder Psychopathology. Eating Disorders, Volume 9, Number 3, pp. 251-259(9)

Using food to fill a feeling of emptiness

Grandma used to take me to the park and we had lots of fun. Since grandpa died, she doesn't want to go. We just stay home and eat cookies, pizza, and cake. Grandma is very fat and always looks sad.

Speaking with your child

Are you upset because grandma doesn't take you to the park? Why do you think she is sad? Do you miss your grandpa? Do you think grandma also misses him?

FACTS People overeat to fill a void. Rather than allow themselves to feel emotions they eat large amounts to "self-medicate" their feelings to deal with life's problems.

Depression and anxiety is often experienced by obese/morbidly obese people and certain *antidepressant medication(s) along with *psychotherapy can be very helpful. *Selective serotonin reuptake inhibitors (SSRIs) are often prescribed by doctors to people with eating disorders. Other antidepressant medication may also be prescribed.

It is very IMPORTANT to consistently communicate with the doctor about past medical history, medications, expected life changes. Also after taking medications for awhile, tell the doctor about any side effects. When a medication is prescribed, ask your doctor:

- The name of the medication, and what is it supposed to do?
- How and when to take it, and when to stop taking it?
- Foods, drinks, other medications, or activities to avoid while taking this medication?
- What are the side effects, and what to do if they occur?
- Is there any written information available about the medication?

GLOSSARY WORDS:

- ***Antidepressant medication** - it is used by psychiatrists and other physicians to help patients get relief from sadness or depression.

- ***Psychotherapy** - a special relationship between a mental health professional and a person to help resolve difficulties in coping with life's problems.

- ***Selective Serotonin Reuptake Inhibitors (SSRIs)** - a class of antidepressant medication that increases serotonin, a chemical responsible for communication between nerves in the brain.

*Genetics

My auntie, my uncle and, and my cousin are overweight. Mama told me that being overweight can be inherited.

Speaking with your child

How do you feel about your weight now? Why do you think Auntie and Johnny are so big? Do you think you are big also? Would you like to learn different ways of eating so we don't get heavy and stay healthy.

FACTS

Genetic *predisposition to obesity and morbid obesity has been widely researched. Slightly overweight children age 10-14 with at least one overweight or obese parent were reported to have a 79% likelihood of being overweight in adulthood, according to statistics from the American Obesity Association[3]. Although genetics is a major factor, most experts agree the increase in processed foods and *sedentary lifestyles are also important factors.

GLOSSARY WORDS:

*Genetics - inherited traits among family members.
*Predisposition - a tendency to develop a similar trait.
*Sedentary - used to sitting or having little activity.

3. The American Obesity Association
    http://www.obesity.org/subs/fastfacts/obesity_youth.shtml

Diabetes

Mommy has ***diabetes**. Some people need shots for diabetes but mommy only takes pills every day.

Speaking with your child

How can you help mommy take care of herself? Do you want to eat healthier and exercise regularly with mommy? Are you worried that you could get diabetes, too?

FACTS

According to the International Diabetes Foundation (IDF), 246 million people worldwide have diabetes and expect the number to reach 380 million by 2025. Approximately 80% percent of those who develop ***type 2 diabetes** are overweight or obese.   In the last 20 years, obesity among children and adults has risen nearly 50% according to IDF[4].

There are medications that may be used for weight loss for people with type 2 diabetes and other serious risk factors and/or medical conditions that are often linked to obesity[4]. These medications, as with any medications would need to be prescribed and monitored by a medical doctor.

GLOSSARY WORDS:

* **Diabetes** - a disease caused by a disorder in the pancreas, in which not enough insulin is produced and sugar cannot be processed properly.

* **Type 2 Diabetes** - non-insulin dependent diabetes. This form of diabetes may be managed with medication(s), diet and exercise.

4.   International Diabetes Foundation
     http://healthlinks.mcw.edu/article941223597.html

Weight Loss Surgery

*Bariatric Surgery

Granddad had an operation on his stomach. Nana says now he will lose weight.

Speaking with your child

It is scary to be in the hospital but your Grandad will feel much better now. We have to help him when he gets home. What can we all do together that will help everyone stay fit, eat better and exercise?

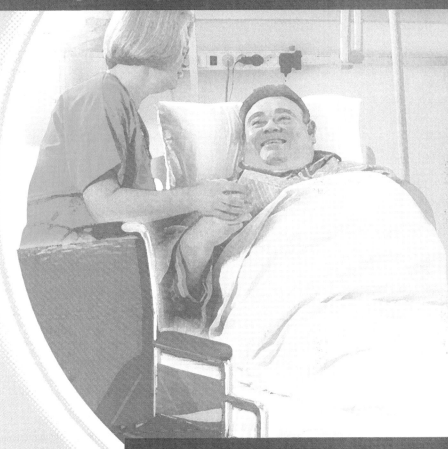

GLOSSARY WORDS:

* **Weight Loss Surgery or Bariatric Surgery** - a gastric procedure to reduce food intake or calories and it is sometimes used to treat morbid obesity.
* **Morbid obesity** - 100 lbs. or more over ideal body weight or Body Mass Index (BMI) of 40 or higher.

FACTS

There are several types of surgery to treat *morbid obesity. In most cases the surgeon alters the stomach or small intestine to make it impossible to eat too much without feeling unpleasant side effects. This usually leads to an initial large weight loss. The patient needs to learn to eat right and exercise before and after the surgery to prevent regaining weight.

Obsession with dieting, calories, & control

I wish I could talk to mom but she's always thinking about other things. She doesn't listen to me. I want to tell her about my day at school but she doesn't hear me.

Speaking with your child

Are you sad because your mom doesn't listen to you?
Do you think she ignores you?
Do you feel whatever mom is thinking is more important than you are?

GLOSSARY WORDS:

*   ***Obsessive** - a repetitive and persistent thought, action, or ritual that is believed to occur as a mechanism for controlling or relieving anxiety.
*   ***Compulsive** - a strong and repetitive urge to act or behave in a certain way. It is often a way of relieving anxiety that results from conflicting ideas and wishes that cannot be directly expressed.
*   ***Rituals** - a formal act or set of acts done by ceremony; doing an act or behavior the exact way each time.
*   ***Dominate** - exercising controlling power over someone or something.

18

FACTS

*Obsessive - ***compulsive** calorie counting, rigid ***eating rituals**, and controlling behaviors are typically exhibited by individuals with Anorexia Nervosa. These behaviors begin to ***dominate** and preoccupy the individual's life to the point that there is little time for daily routines, work, and relationships

Refusal To Maintain Minimum Normal Body Weight

My sister Alex doesn't like to eat her meals. My mum makes her come to the table, but Alex just looks angry and doesn't eat her food. Doesn't she like mom's cooking?

Speaking with your child

Why do you think Alex doesn't want to eat? Do you think she is full? Do you think she is heavy or thin? Are you worried about her?

GLOSSARY WORDS:

* **Restricting** - when an individual intentionally and drastically decreases the amount of food eaten for the purpose of weight loss.
* **Eating disorder** - a person who has an unhealthy relationship with food and has recurring episodes of over or under eating, distress regarding body size, negatively compares one's body to others, over exercising, taking medication to loose or maintain weight.

19

FACTS

*Restricting food intake is one of the most common symptoms of AN. This behavior is a result of the person with an *eating disorder having an intense fear of gaining weight despite being underweight. To have AN, a person's body weight must be at least 15% below what is expected for the age, gender, and height of the person.

Distorted Perception of Body Weight/Shape

Mommy and I used to go swimming all the time. Now, she never wants to go swimming, she says she looks fat. I think my mommy is beautiful and she is not fat.

Speaking with your child

Why does mommy always think she looks so fat? Would you like to go swimming with your mommy again? Do you wish that mommy had more energy to play with you?

FACTS

Individuals with AN experience a *distorted view of their body weight and or shape. They see themselves as larger than their actual size, therefore feeling unattractive. They may resort to *purging, using and abusing laxatives, water pills, or enemas.

GLOSSARY WORDS:

* **Distorted** - to have an inaccurate view of self, someone or something.
* **Purging** - self-induced vomiting to rid unwanted food/calories.

20

*Excessive Exercising

Tio Roberto is my mom's brother. Tio used to take me to the movies and the park, but he doesn't have time now. He always has to go to the gym. I wish we could do things together again.

Speaking with your child

Do you wish you could spend more time with Tio? Do you think the gym is more important to him than you are?

FACTS

People with AN have a tendency to diet and exercise to an extreme. Exercising could occur 2-4 times or more per day and could absorb a significant part of the individual's day, leaving little time for regular daily living and relationships with others. Over time, *excessive exercise can result in physical and medical complications. Some of the medical problems may result in: *degenerative joint disease, *arthritis, ankle, knee, and hip problems, back and neck injuries.

GLOSSARY WORDS:

* **Excessive** - an amount or quantity beyond what is needed, desired, or appropriate.

* **Degenerative** - growing less healthy over time

* **Arthritis** - inflammation of a joint(s) causing pain, swelling and stiffness.

21

Dressing in layers to hide weight loss

My sister wears lots of sweaters all the time. Even when it's hot outside, she wears long sleeve shirts and long pants. I wonder if she is cold. Maybe she is sick.

Speaking with your child

Why do you think your sister wears all these clothes? Do you think she's hiding something? Do you think she's sick?

FACTS

People with AN have little body fat and they tend to get cold in even warm temperatures. They may wear long sleeve shirts and long pants all the time. However these people also choose these clothes to cover up their very thin bodies. This is an attempt to continue their *starvation process. A common statement made by individuals with AN is: "I hate my body" which equates to "I hate who I am."

GLOSSARY WORDS:

*Starvation - to suffer from prolonged lack of food

Lack of Control

Daddy eats more than anyone I've ever seen. Sometimes I think he can't stop eating. It makes me nervous because he eats really fast. If I eat slowly, he eats my food even when I want it.

Speaking with your child

Daddy has problems and he can't help it that he eats so much. Are you upset at your daddy that he eats your dessert? Do you think you have to eat fast so your daddy won't eat your food?

GLOSSARY WORDS:

*Abnormal - a function usually seen as not working well or maladaptive for the person.

*Carbohydrates - sugars and starches, like cake, cookies, candy, ice cream.

*Fasting - to eat very little or not at all.

FACTS Features of Bulimia Nervosa include eating large amounts of food usually within a two-hour period and making up for the weight gain by purging or doing a great deal of exercise. The type of food eaten during a binge may vary, but it usually includes an *abnormal amount of sweet, high-calorie *carbohydrates, such as, ice cream or cake. There are two types of BN. The first is the purging type, which includes: self-induced vomiting, the misuse of laxatives, or diuretics (water pills).

The second type of BN is the non-purging type. The individual makes up for weight gain by *fasting or too much exercise, but does not regularly purge. A person with BN experiences loss of control when overeating and feels like they can't stop eating or control what or how much they eat.

Secretive Eating

My papa is always hungry. Sometimes, I wake up and he is eating all by himself in the kitchen. He gets angry if I tell him that I am hungry too. He doesn't like me to eat with him at night.

Speaking with your child

Are you upset that you can't have a late night snack with papa?
What happens if you get hungry at night?
Do you wonder why he eats at night?
Even when your papa yells at you, he is not angry with you. Papa has an eating problem and that is why he eats at night.

GLOSSARY WORDS:

*Isolate - being kept apart from others.

*Intimate - a strong sense of physical and emotional closeness that permits mutual caring about the most personal feelings and needs.

FACTS

Secretive eating is common with individuals who have BN. They plan times when they can be alone to binge-eat, and they tend to *isolate themselves and have difficulty with *intimate relationships. They tend to have a strong need for others' approval yet can be overly sensitive to criticism.

24

Normal Weight

My family eats dinner together and everyone talks about what they did at school or work. It's my favorite time because we're all together. Sometimes after dinner, my sister goes into the bathroom and I hear her vomiting.

Speaking with your child

Why does your sister vomit after dinner? Do you think maybe she's sick? Do you think it's gross? Have you ever asked her why she vomits after dinner?

GLOSSARY WORDS:

*Compensate - a way of thinking in which one tries to make up for something they did or said that is undesirable.

FACTS

Although individuals who have BN can be underweight or overweight, they usually fall into the normal weight range because of the purging or non-purging behaviors. They do this to *compensate for what they've eaten. These behaviors are primarily how BN maintain their normal weight.

25

Medication

Poppy used to look sad all the time. He never wanted to play with me. Now we go fishing, we play ball and he looks happier, too.
He says the doctor gave him medicine that helps him feel better.

Speaking with your child

Are you happy that poppy plays with you now? How can you tell your poppy is feeling better? What kind of activities do you like to do with poppy?

FACTS

*Antidepressant medication along with *psychotherapy have proved to have some positive effect for people with certain eating disorders. It is common for people with eating disorders to experience depression and or anxiety. Often doctors prescribe *selective serotonin reuptake inhibitors (SSRI's) such as fluoxetine, sertraline, paroxetine and fluvoxamine. Other antidepressant medication may also be prescribed.

GLOSSARY WORDS:

* **Antidepressant medication** - prescribed drugs to help patients achieve relief from symptoms of depression.
* **Psychotherapy** - a specialized, interaction between a mental health professional and a patient in which a therapeutic relationship is established to help resolve difficulties in coping.
* **Selective Serotonin Reuptake Inhibitors (SSRI's)** - a class of antidepressant drugs that help to increase serotonin, a chemical responsible for communication between nerves in the brain.

Individual Therapy

Mama goes to see a "therapist" who helps her to have a healthier relationship with food. She also goes to see a nutritionist to learn to eat the right foods. Mama also exercises and sometimes we go biking together. Mama feels better now and she has a lot of friends too, who help each other to stay healthy.

Speaking with your child

Why does Mama have a healthier relationship with food? Do you have a healthy relationship with food also? Is mama happier now? Do you eat healthier foods also? What new food are you eating now?

FACTS

An important part of *treatment and *recovery for individuals with eating disorders is talk therapy and proper nutrition. Talk therapy can help a person deal with feelings of low self-worth/esteem, loneliness, depression, anxiety, personal and family problems, childhood abuse or trauma. Talk therapy helps a person become aware, identify, and deal with past issues and the painful emotions that are often attached to them and the eating disorder can often be put in remission.

GLOSSARY WORDS:

* **Treatment** - correcting a disorder, disease, or problem.
* **Recovery** - a process of regaining control of ones life following addiction to food, alcohol, drugs, etc. People in recovery often belong to 12-Step Programs or support groups.

27

Some Other Helpful Disciplines

1). Medical check-up:

A physical examination is very important for people with eating disorders. Whether the behaviors are that of someone who binge eats, or who is Bulimic, or Anorexic, makes no difference; they have had an unhealthy relationship with food that could lead to different physical problems.

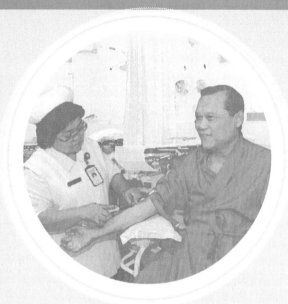

2). Group therapy:

Participating in a group therapy process has shown to be very helpful for people with eating disorders. A professional that specializes in eating disorders leads the group with topics related to eating disorders and allows its members to express openly their thoughts and feelings.

3). Psychiatric Visits:

Some people with eating disorders feel depressed or anxious. A psychiatrist is a doctor specializing in the prevention and treatment of mental and emotional problems. The psychiatrist can choose the correct medication for the eating disordered person to feel better.

4). Nutritionist or Dietician:

A nutritionist or dietician is a health professional with special training in healthy eating, who can offer help with better choices of food and drink and the correct amounts. Seeing a nutritionist could help change the relationship with food to a healthier and more balanced one.

Some Other Helpful Disciplines

5). 12-Step Recovery Programs:

The 12-Step Programs are one of the many avenues designed to help in the recovery from addictions or compulsive behaviors. Members of 12-Step Programs attend meetings regularly and share about their experience, strength and hope in regard to their particular addiction or compulsive behavior. The fellowship found in the 12-Step Programs is very supportive and helpful to its members, promoting abstinence from the problematic behavior or addiction.

6). Family Therapy:

An eating disorder can affect the entire family In family therapy each member can have the opportunity to express what they think and feel in a safe, nurturing environment provided by a professional therapist. This process can be healing for the entire family and allow family members to experience an even closer bond in their relationships.

How Can You Make A Difference?

How can you be a positive support for your loved one with an eating disorder?

- Learn as much as you can about your loved ones particular eating disorder.
- Participate in different exercises with your loved one.
- Make good food choices yourself.
- Be supportive, especially in the grocery store when choosing which foods and drinks to buy and when eating out in restaurants.
- Praise and encourage your loved one when he or she makes good food choices.
- When possible, participate in family therapy and openly talk about what is really going on and what you are really feeling and thinking.

What are some of the things that you've learned about in this book that your loved one with an eating disorder could do to be healthier and feel better?

- Make good choices with food and amounts of food eaten.
- Exercise.
- Go to therapy.
- Attend 12-Step Meetings for support.
- Go to a doctor for a medical examination.
- Go to a Nutritionist.
- Go to a psychiatrist for medication, if needed.
- Talk about how he/she is feeling.

Worldwide Obesity

Global overweight now rivals underweight

For the first time, the number of overweight individuals around the world rivals the numbers who are underweight. Most worrying is the fact that obese children may die before their parents if action is not taken. Developing nations, including those beset by hunger, are also now troubled by obesity. Obesity is one of the greatest public health challenges of the 21st century and the numbers of those affected continue to rise at an alarming rate, particularly among children.

Overweight children and adolescents are at risk for health problems during their youth and as adults. Overweight children and adolescents are more likely to have risk factors associated with cardiovascular disease (such as high blood pressure, high cholesterol, and Type 2 diabetes) than are other children and adolescents. Overweight children and adolescents are more likely to become obese as adults.

Obesity in the West

USA obesity rates are at epidemic proportions

In the United States, obesity is the most common chronic disease, affecting more than 1 in 4 of all Americans, including children, and its incidence has been steadily increasing for the past 20 years.

- Over 64% of adult Americans are either overweight or obese.
- 76% increase in Type II diabetes in adults 30-40 yrs old since 1990.

- Eight out of 10 over 25's are overweight.
- Children aged 2–5 years, prevalence increased from 5.0% to 13.9%; for those aged 6–11 years, prevalence increased from 6.5% to 18.8%; and for those aged 12–19 years, prevalence increased from 5.0% to 17.4% 1. (NHANES data on the Prevalence of Overweight Among Children and Adolescents: United States, 2003–2004. CDC National Center for Health Statistics, Health E-Stat. (http://www.cdc.gov/nchs/products/pubs/pubd/hestats/overweight).

UK and Europe

- In the UK, over the past 25 years obesity rates among women has tripled from 8% to 24% and rates have quadrupled in men from 6% to 24%.

- In less than six years, 86% of men will be overweight, 50% of which will be obese.

- Within 20 years, 70% of women will be overweight and 50% of these will be obese.

- If trends continue, half the population of the UK will be obese by 2032.

Adult prevalence of obesity by nation in the EU ranges from about 10% in France to about 25% in Greece. World Health Organization (WHO) figures suggest that obesity presents a major public health problem, especially as levels are rising very quickly.

- The International Obesity Taskforce (IOTF) estimates overall European prevalence of childhood overweight to be 24%. This represents an accelerated increase exceeding the predicted figure for the year 2010, based on trends from the 1980s (LOBSTEIN T, BAUR L, & UAUY R. Obesity in children and young people: a crisis in public health. Obesity Reviews 2004; volume 5 supplement 1: 4-85).

- In Europe, Australia/New Zealand, the Middle East, and the remaining portions of the Americas, the occurrence of obesity is increasing and is now between 10 and 20 percent.

- There are approximately 74 million school children aged 4-18 in the EU. Based on prevalence estimates it is possible to calculate that 11.8 million to 16.3 million children are overweight and obese, of which 2.9 million to 4.4million are actually obese.*

- A Conservative estimate for 2005 compared with 2004, indicates that 400,000 – 600,000 more children were overweight, and 80,000 – 130,000 obese.*

- On this basis, there will be over 20 million overweight children in the EC, of which 5 million will be obese within a decade.*

*(European Association for the Study of Obesity)

Sources for help with Eating Disorders

12-Step Programs:

Anorexics and Bulimics Anonymous
Main P.O. Box 125
Edmonton, AB T5J2G9
www.anorexicsandbulimicsanonymousaba.com

Food Addicts Anonymous World Service Office
4623 Forest Hill Blvd., Suite #109-4
West Palm Beach, FL 33415-9120
Fax: 561-967-9815
www.foodaddictsanonymous.org

Overeaters Anonymous World Service Office
P.O. Box 44020
Rio Rancho, NM 87174-4020 USA
Fax: (505) 891-4320
www.oa.org

Treatment Facilities:

Avalon Eating Disorder Treatment Center
346 Harris Hill Road
Williamsville, NY 14221
Fax: (716) 839-2058
Info@avalon-centers.com

Info for Eating Disorders in New Zealand:
http://www.nzhealth.net.nz/diet/eating.dis.html

The International Eating Disorder Centre
119-121 Wendover Road
Aylesbury
Bucks, HP21 9LW, UK
webenquiry@eatingdisordercentre.co.uk

Rader Programs
www.raderprograms.com

The Renfrew Center Foundation
475 Spring Lane
Philadelphia, PA 19128
Fax: (215) 482-2695
E-Mail: foundation@renfrew.org

References

1. American Psychiatric Association. (1994). Diagnostic and statistical manual of mental   disorders (4th ed.). Washington, DC: Author

2. Barker, R. L. (2003). The Social Work Dictionary. (5th ed.). Washington, DC: NASW Press

3. Department of Health and Human Services Center for Disease Control and Prevention http://www.cdc.gov/nccdphp/dnpa/obesity/trend/index.htm

4. International Diabetes Foundation http://healthlinks.mcw.edu/article941223597.html

5. Jongsma, A. & Pererson, L. (1995) The Complete Psychotherapy Treatment Planner. New York: Wiley-Interscience Publication

6. Olshansky, S.J., D. J. Passaro, Hershow, R.C. Layden, J. (2005). A Potential Decline in Life Expectancy in the United States in the 21st Century. New England Journal of Medicine, 352, 1138-1146.

7. The American Obesity Association http://www.obesity.org/subs/fastfacts/obesity_youth.shtml

8. www.heartstats.org British Heart Foundation Statistics Website

9. Annual Report on the Rare Diseases and Conditions Research Activities of the National Institutes of Health FY 2000

10. World Health Organization http://www.who.int/

11. Medscape Medical News http://www.medscape.com/viewarticle/537382

12. Stark, C.A. (2001). Food Addicts Anonymous 12-Step Recovery Book, 15-19.